Step back in time with the PM dinosaurs as you learn Queensland Modern Cursive handwriting.

My name is

My teacher's name is

My school is

Are you ready to write?

Posture

Is your back resting against the chair?

Are your feet flat on the floor?

Paper position

left-handed

Are you holding the paper steady with your non-writing hand?

right-handed

Pencil grip

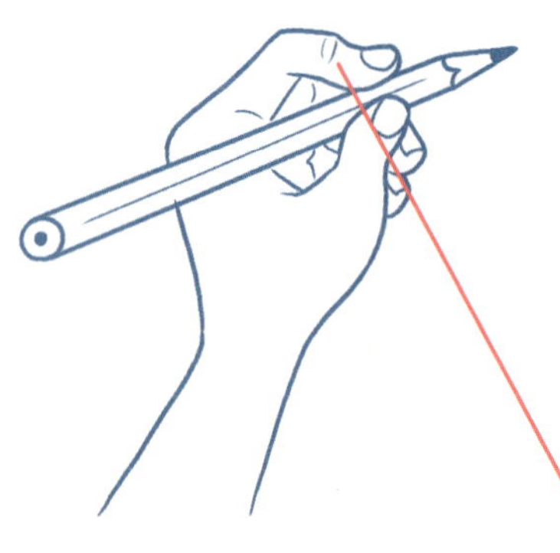

Is there only one finger on top of the pencil?

Left-handers, hold your pencil a little further up so you can see your handwriting!

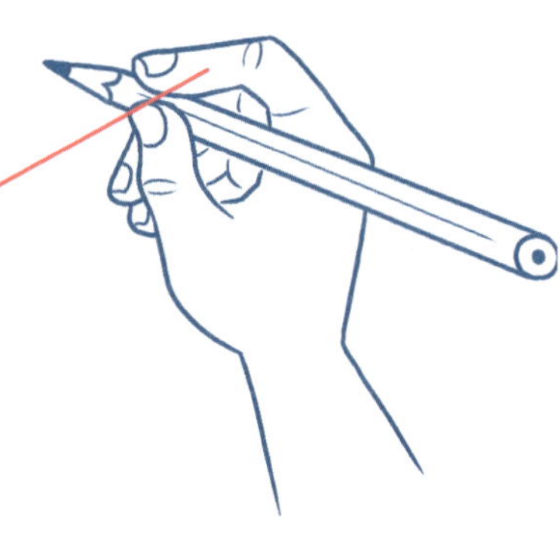

Straight-line letters

Try these straight-line letter patterns. Start at the red dots. Follow the arrows.

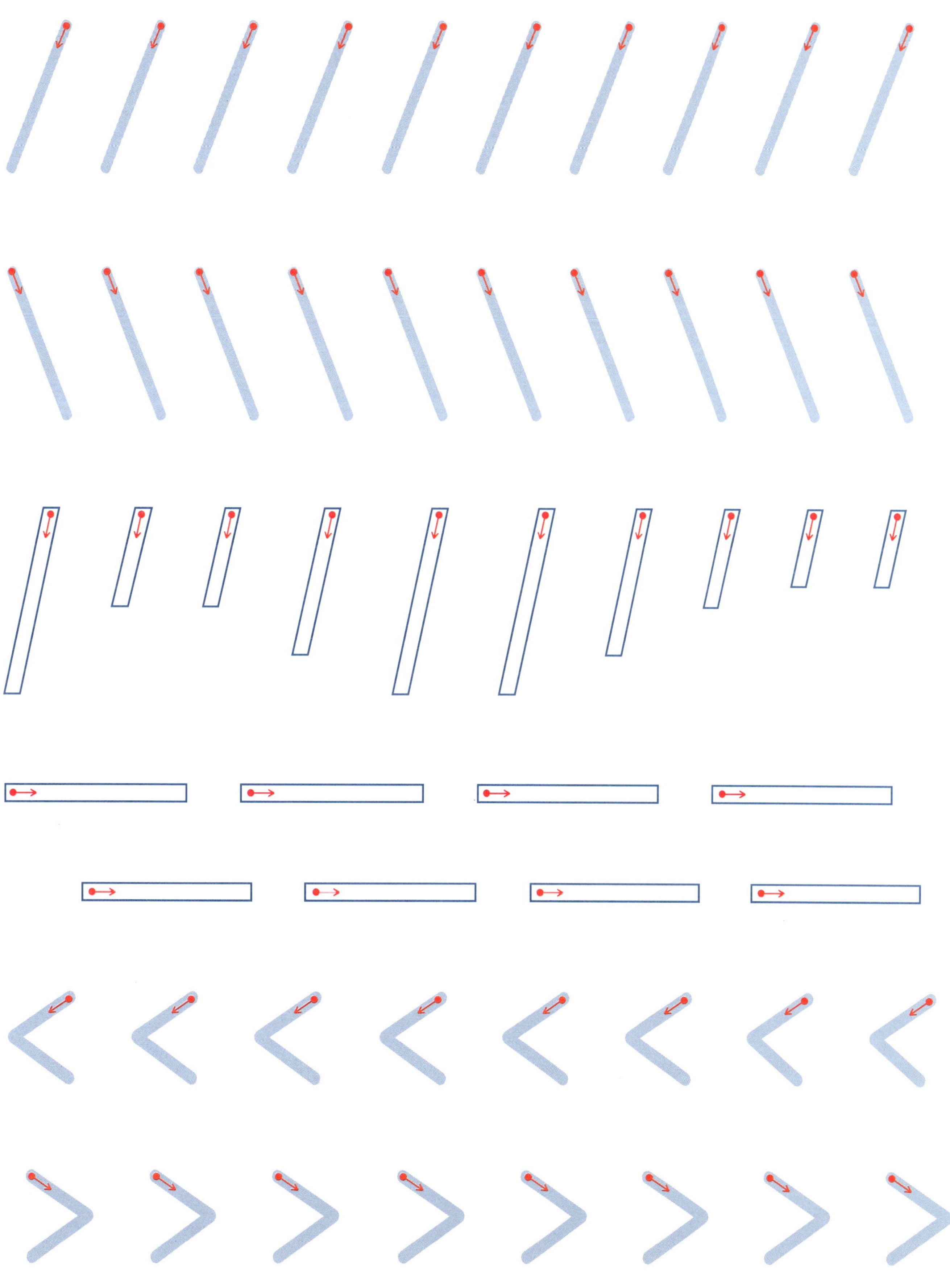

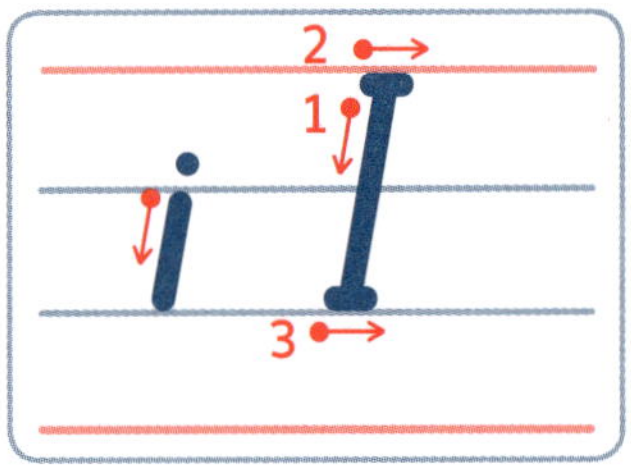

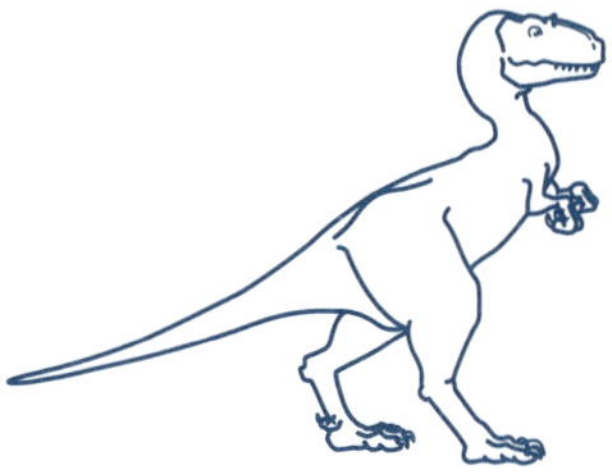

i I

Trace.

Trace and copy.

i i i i i i i

i

I I I

idea important indeed

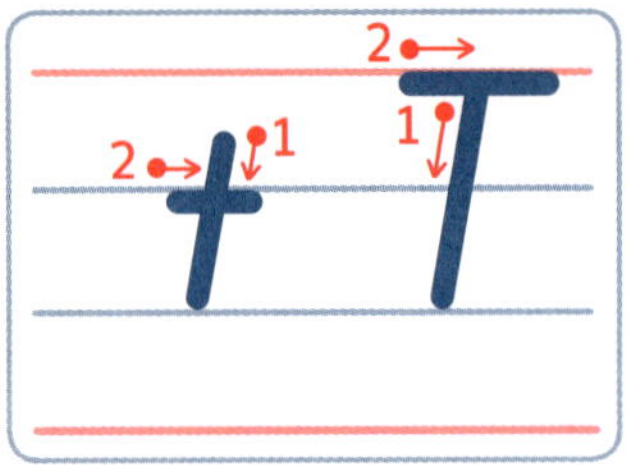

t T

Trace.

Trace and copy.

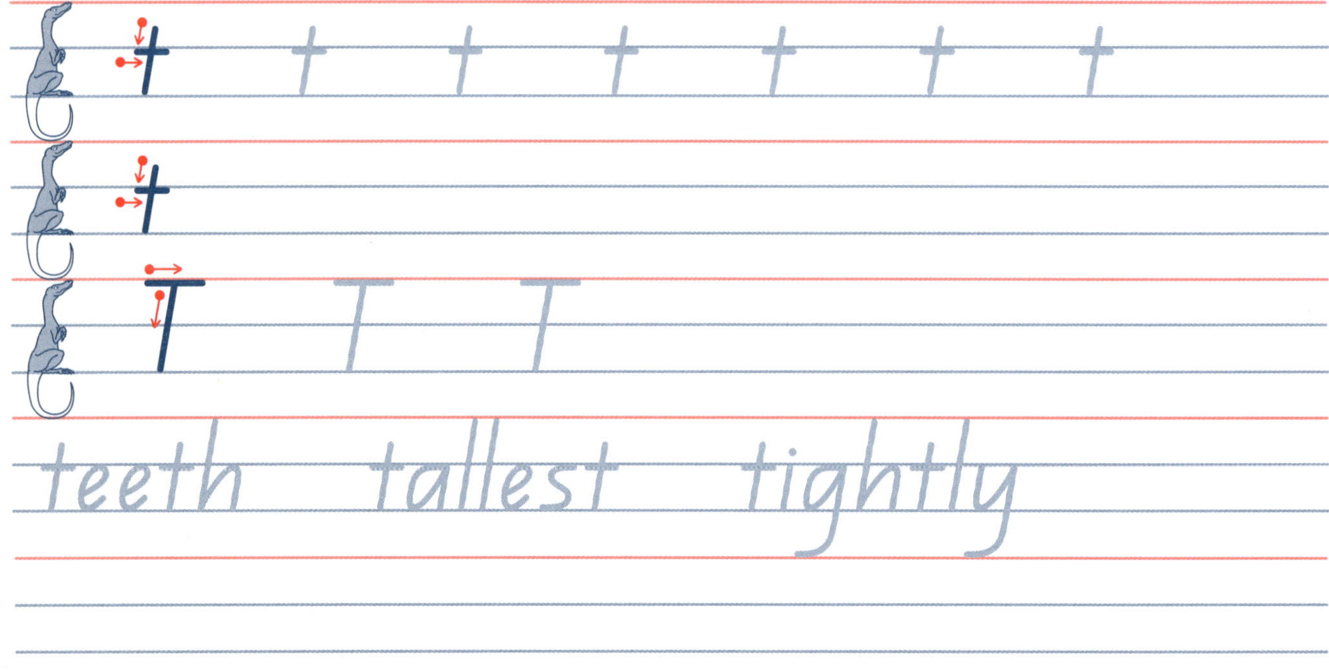

l L
Trace.
Trace and copy.
little lizard leaves
1 x 2 1 X 2
Trace.
Trace and copy.
boxes x-ray six fix

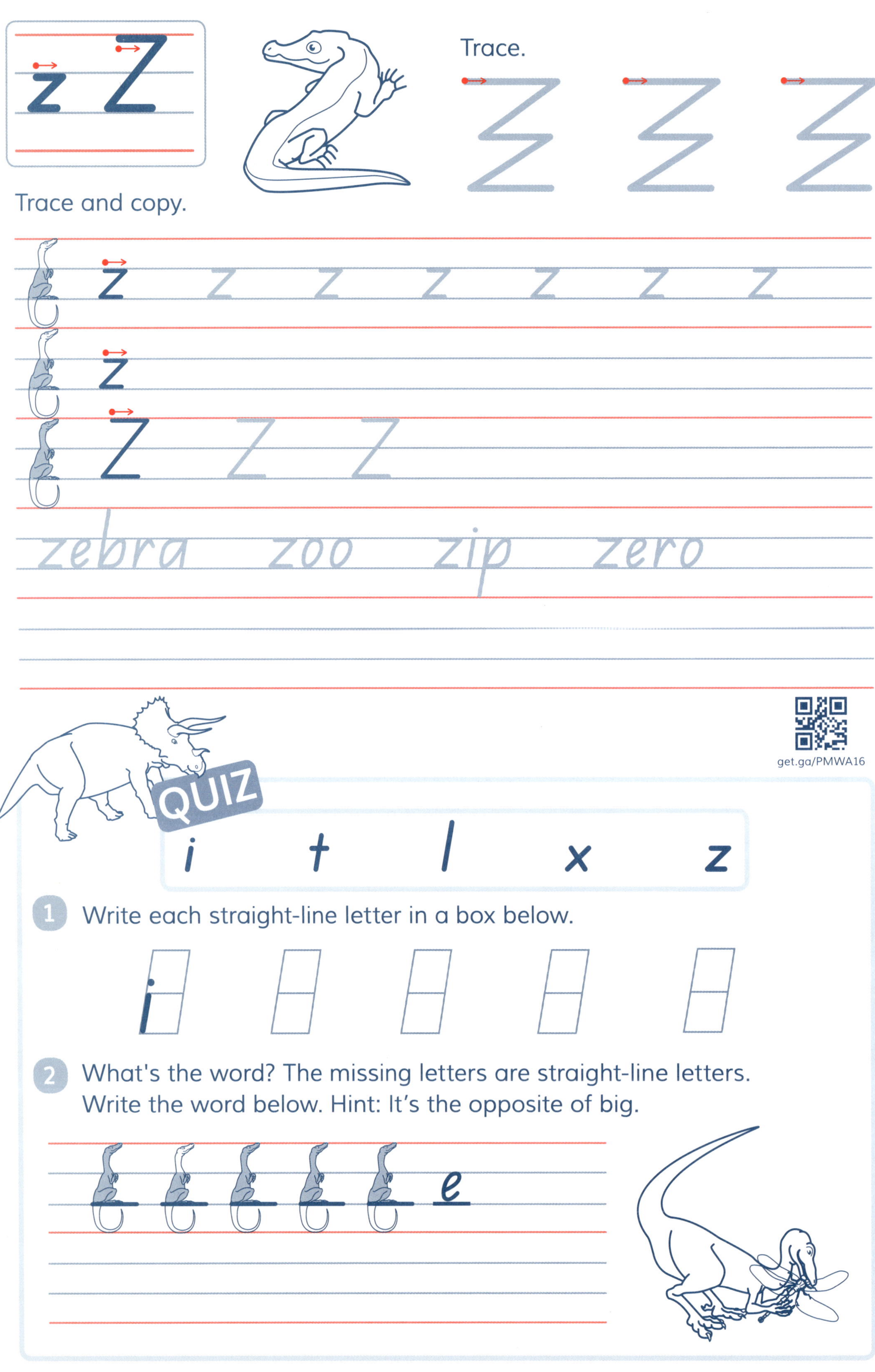
z Z
Trace.
Z Z Z
Trace and copy.
z z z z z z z
z
Z Z Z
zebra zoo zip zero
get.ga/PMWA16
QUIZ
i t l x z
1 Write each straight-line letter in a box below.
i
2 What's the word? The missing letters are straight-line letters.
Write the word below. Hint: It's the opposite of big.
e

Clockwise letters

Try these clockwise letter patterns. Start at the red dots. Follow the arrows.

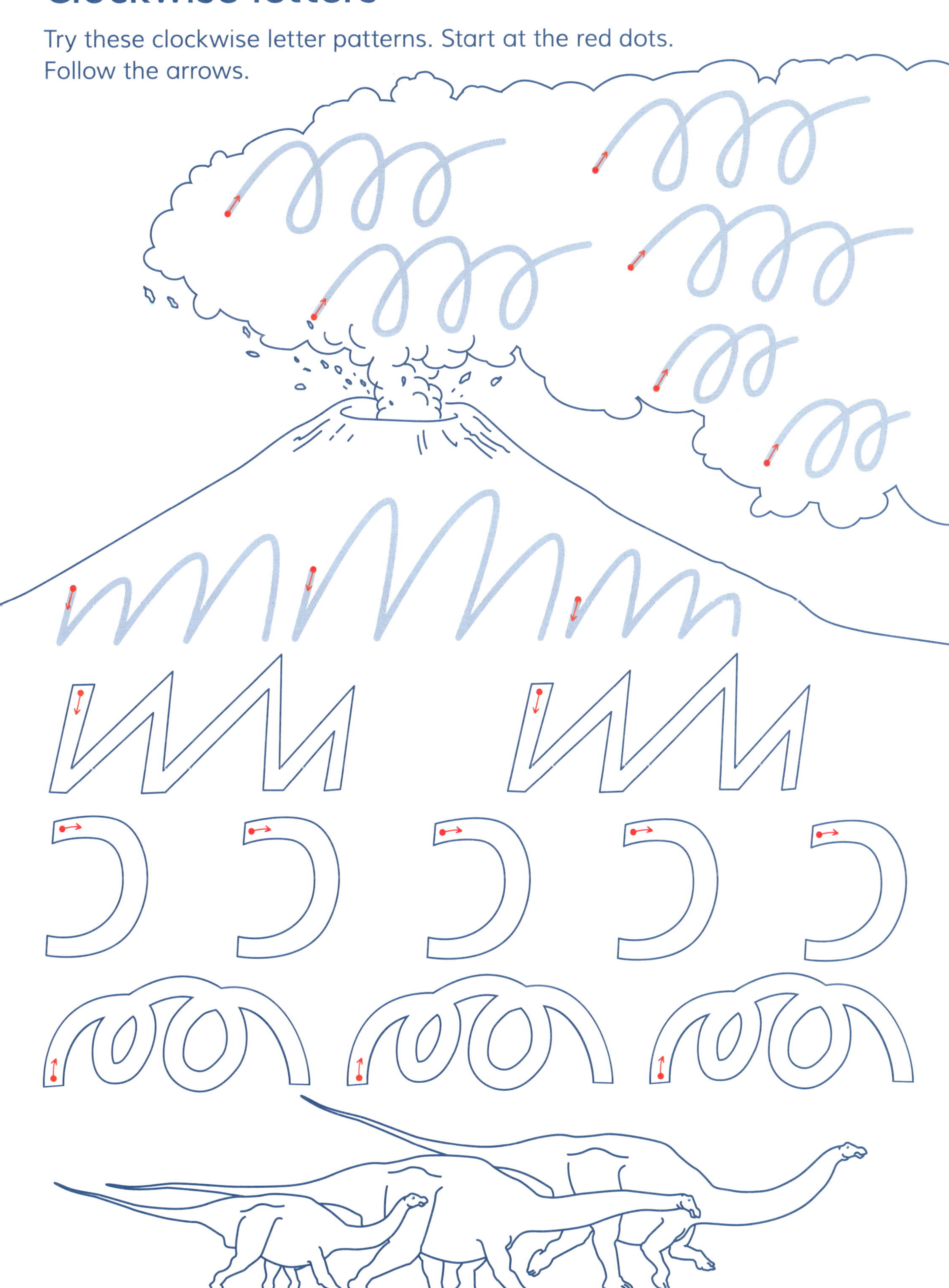

Trace.

Trace and copy.

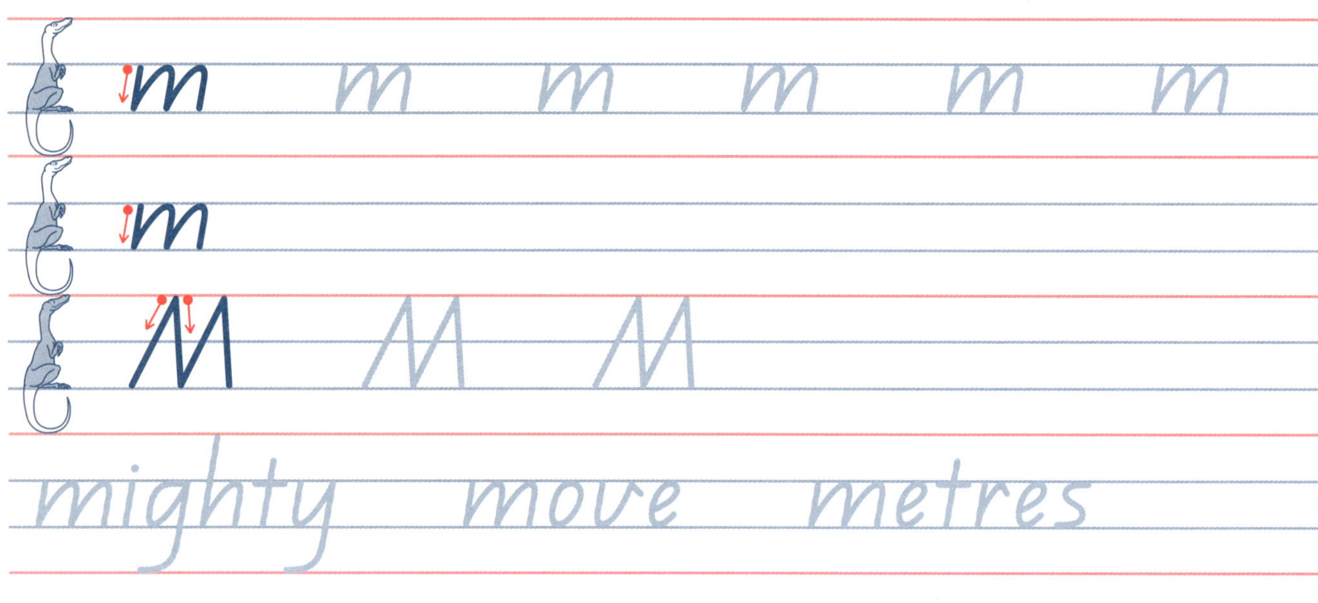

Trace.

Trace and copy.

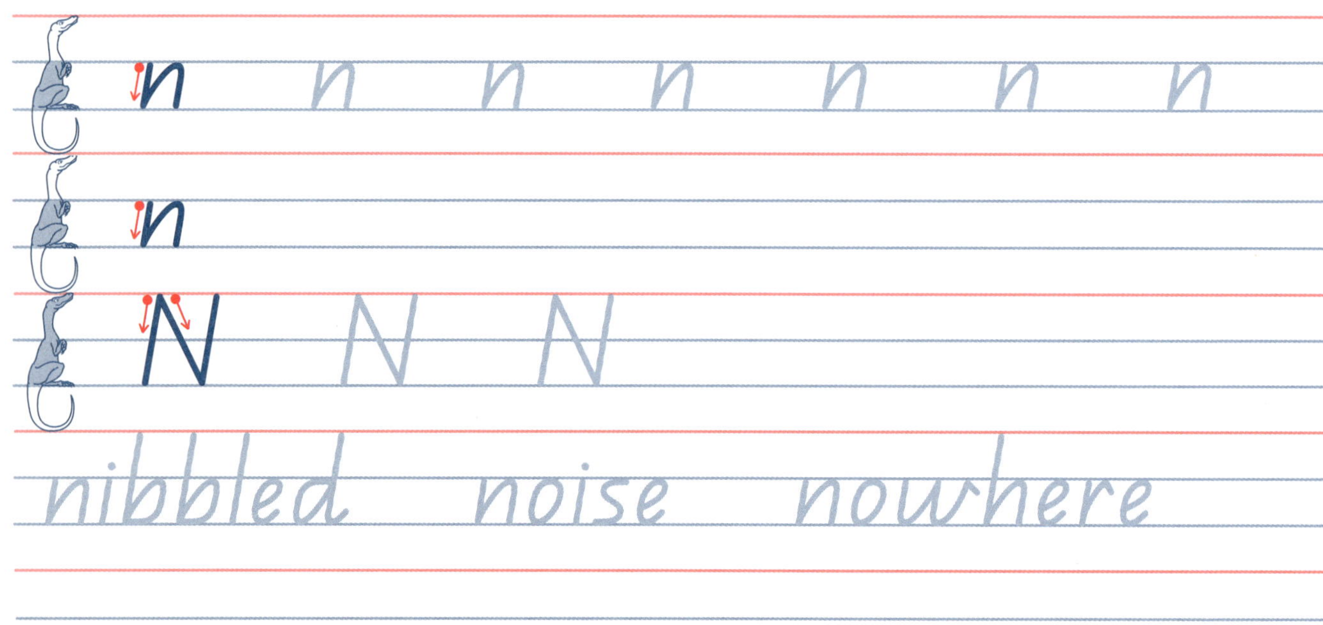

h H
1
2
3
Trace.
Trace and copy.
h
h
H
hungry head huge
r R
1
2
Trace.
Trace and copy.
r
r
R
river roared rain

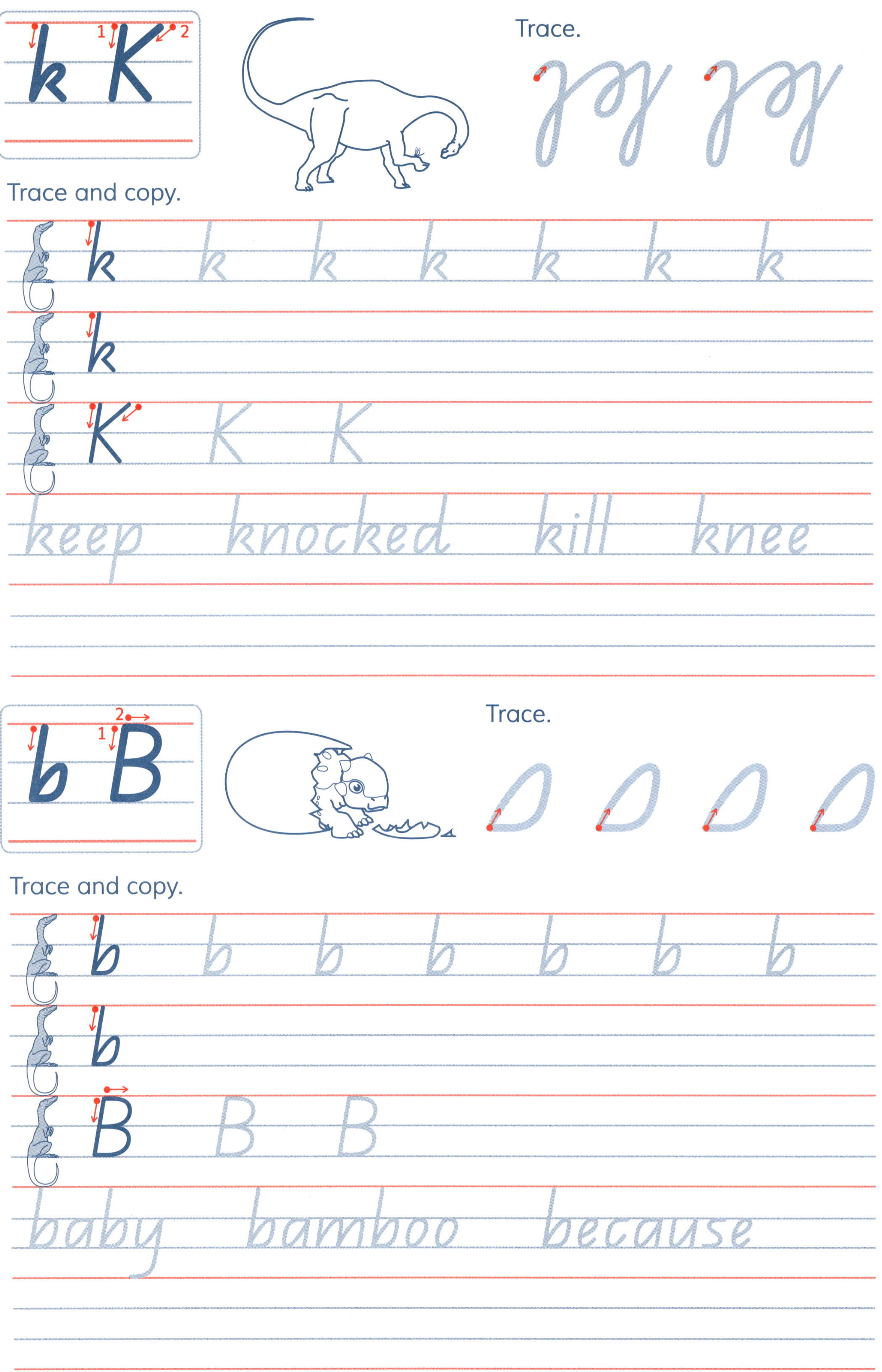

k K
Trace.
Trace and copy.
k
k
K
keep knocked kill knee
b B
Trace.
Trace and copy.
b
b
B
baby bamboo because

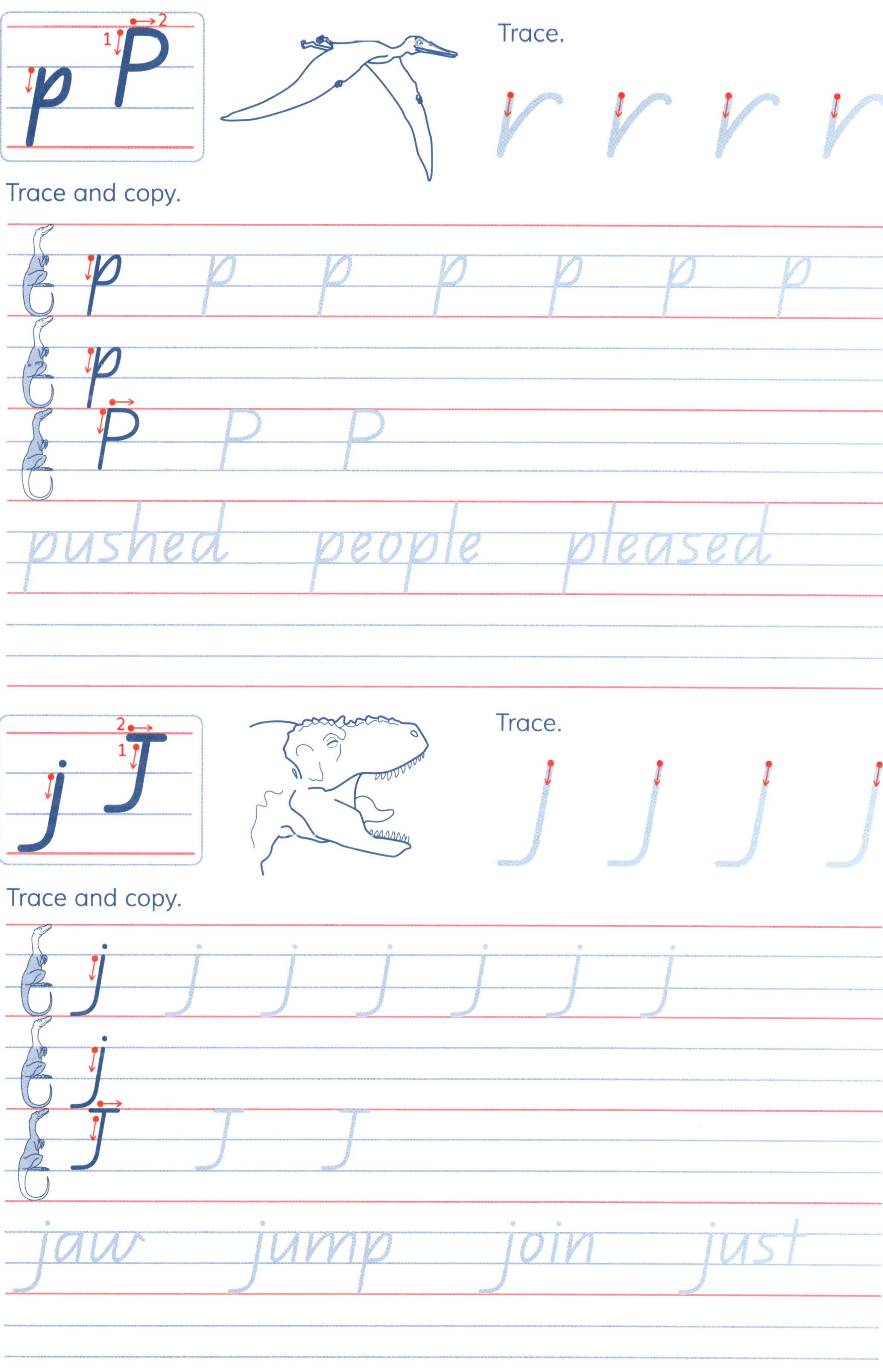
p P
1
2
Trace.
r r r r
Trace and copy.
p p p p p p p
p
P P P
pushed people pleased
j J
1
2
Trace.
j j j j
Trace and copy.
j j j j j j j
j
J J J
jaw jump join just

Trace and copy the sentences. Circle your neatest word.

Tyrannosaurus Rex

had powerful back legs.

It ran after its prey.

1. Colour the wedges.

h m b k n r

2. What clockwise letters are missing from the words below?

Another word for huge: e_o__ _ous

Opposite of evening: _o_ _i_g

Anti-clockwise letters

Try these anti-clockwise letter patterns. Start at the red dots. Follow the arrows.

Trace.

uu uu

Trace and copy.

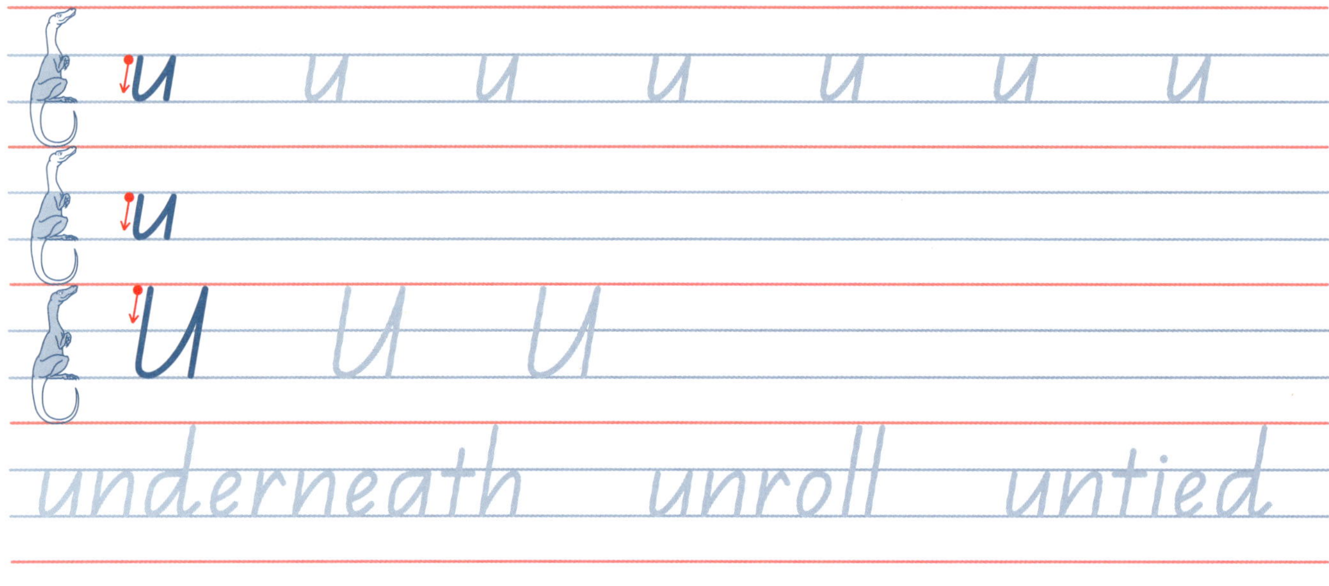

Trace.

iee iee

Trace and copy.

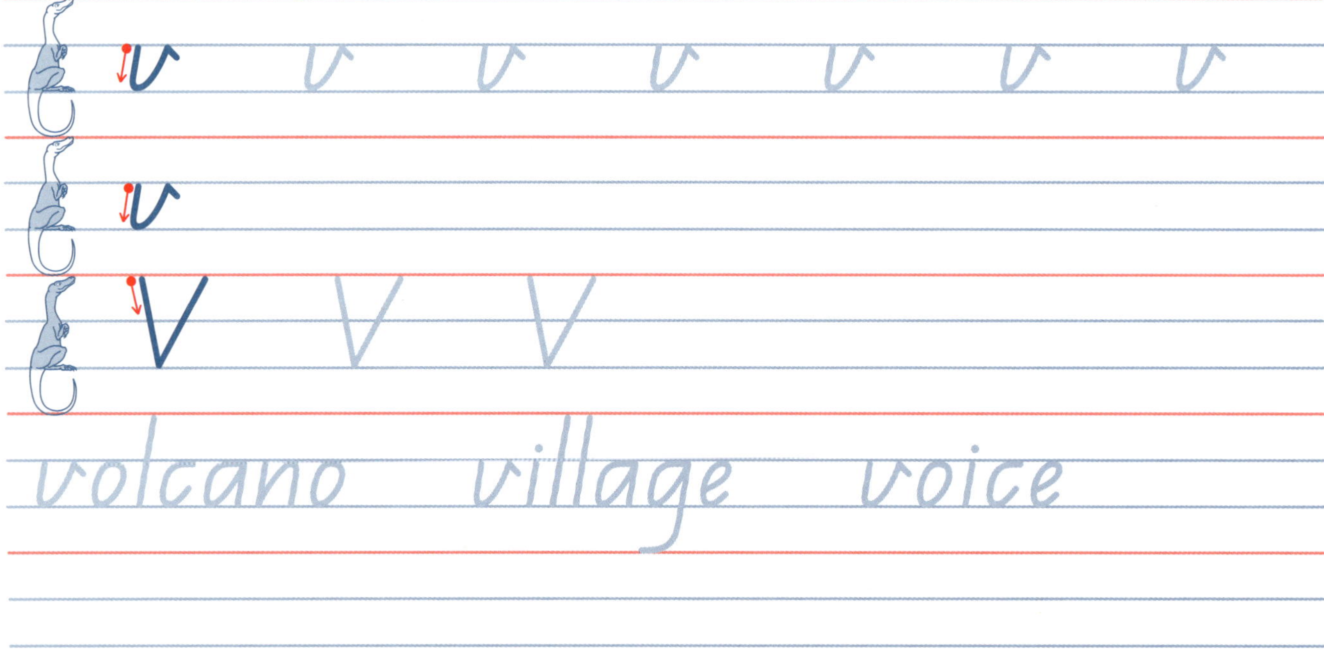

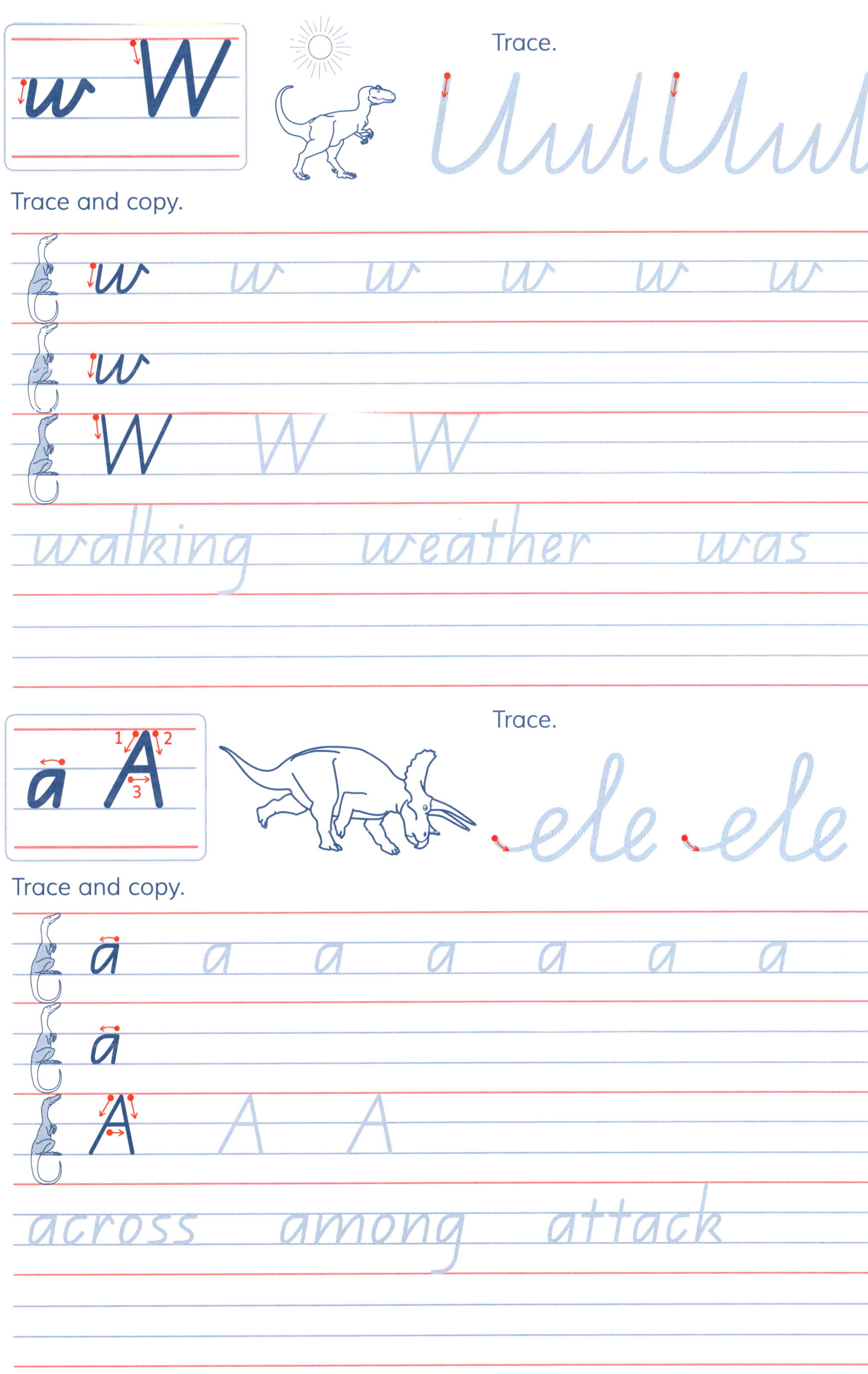
w W
Trace.
Trace and copy.
w w w w w w
w
W W W
walking weather was
a A
Trace.
ele ele
Trace and copy.
a a a a a a a
a
A A A
across among attack

c C
Trace.
Trace and copy.
c
c
C
chase crocodile climbed
d D
Trace.
Trace and copy.
d
d
D
dinosaur danger deep

q Q
1
2
Trace.
Trace and copy.
q q q q q q q
q
Q Q Q
quickly quietly quite
f F
1
2
1
2
3
Trace.
Trace and copy.
f f f f f f f
f
F F F
ferns forest feathers

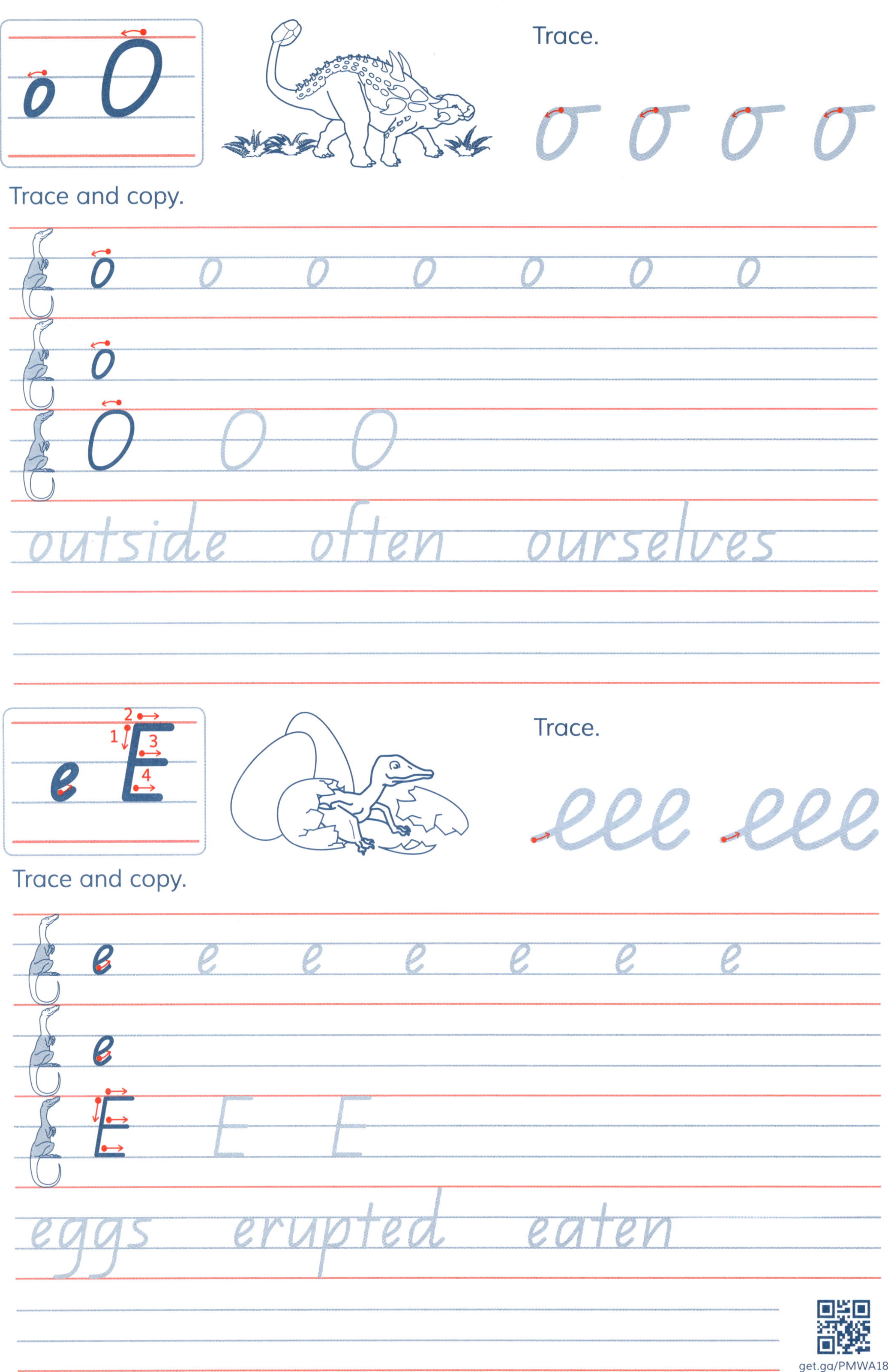

o O

Trace.

o o o o

Trace and copy.

o o o o o o o

o

O O O

outside often ourselves

e E

Trace.

eee eee

Trace and copy.

e e e e e e e

e

E E E

eggs erupted eaten

get.ga/PMWA18

Double-rotation letters

Try these double-rotation letter patterns. Start at the red dots. Follow the arrows.

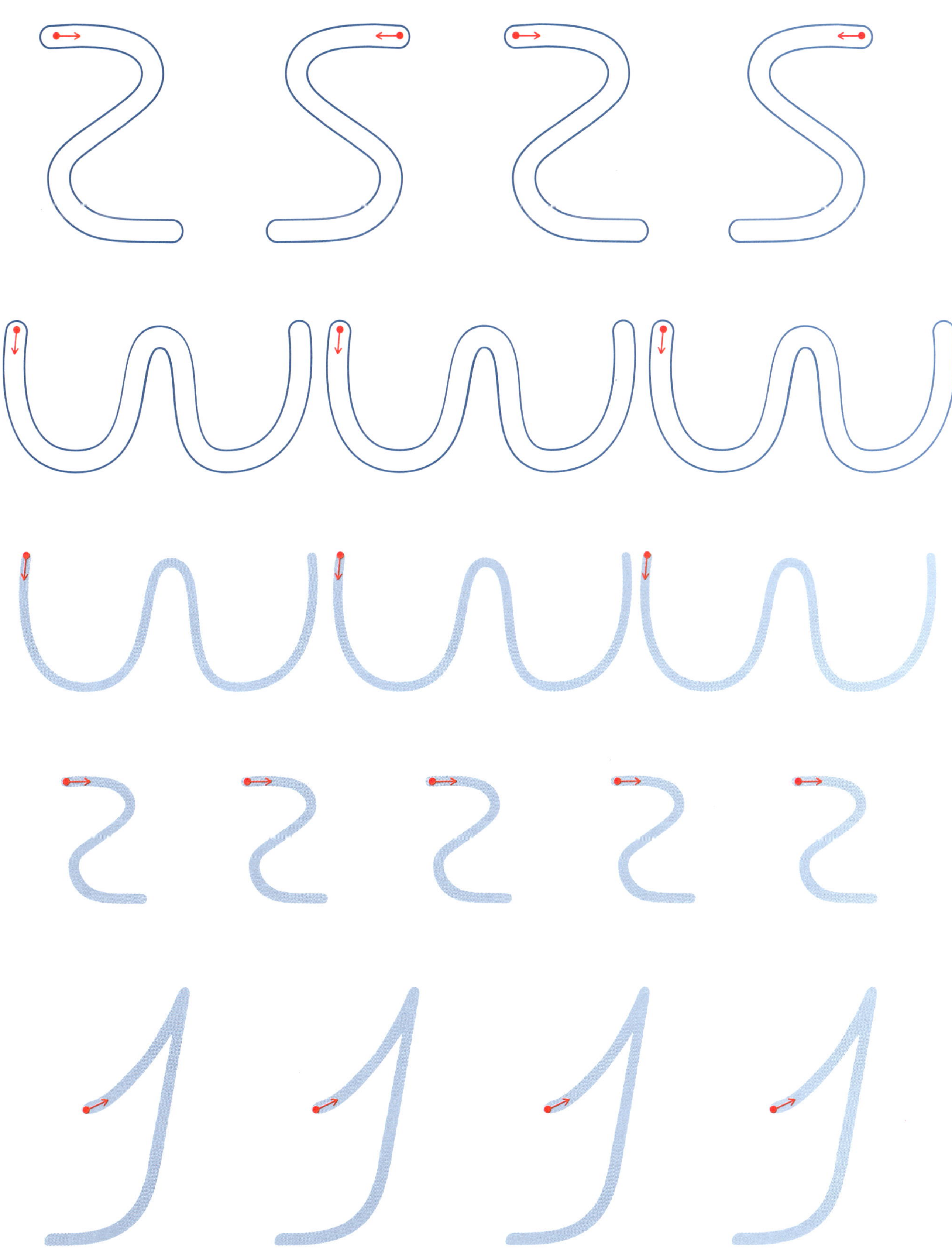

g G
Trace.
Trace and copy.
g g g g g g g
g
G G G
green groan goodnight
y Y
1 2 3
Trace.
Trace and copy.
y y y y y y y
y
Y Y Y
year yesterday yet

Trace.

Trace and copy.

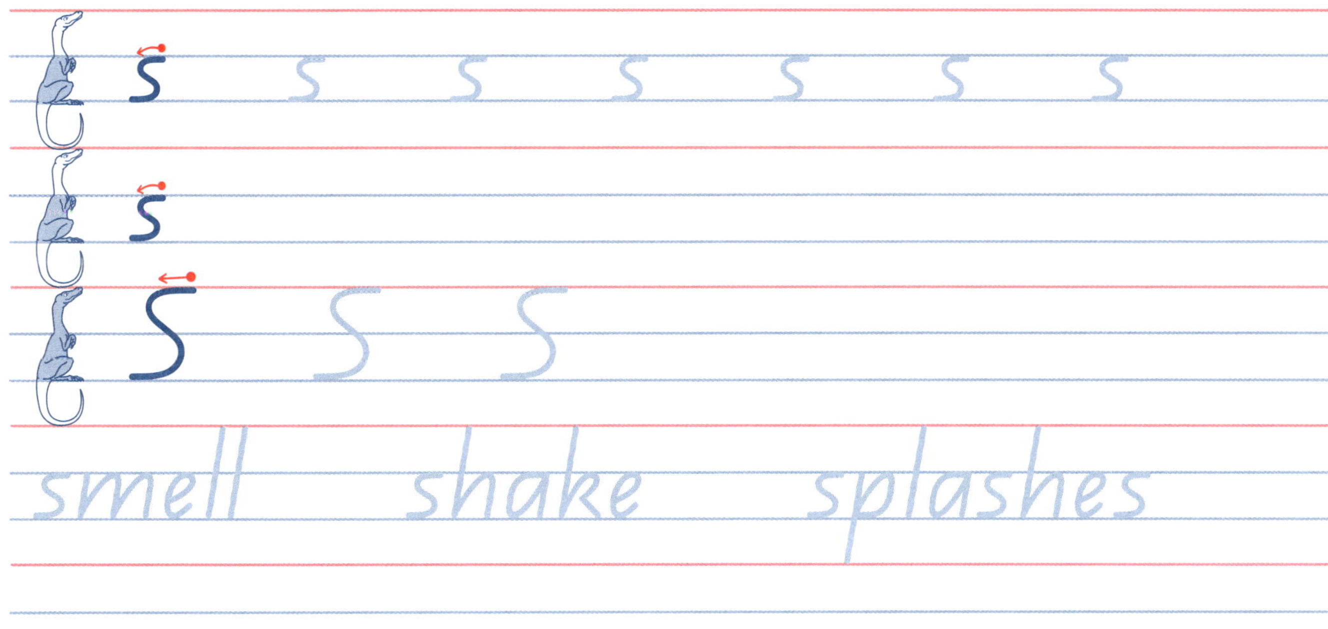

get.ga/PMWA19

Colour the parts of the dinosaur to show what type of letter it is.

Self-assessment

My Beginner's Alphabet is:

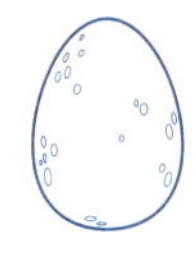

getting there.

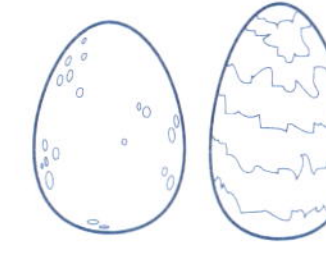

very good.

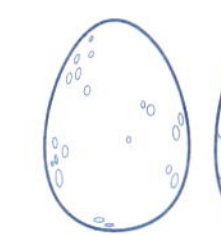

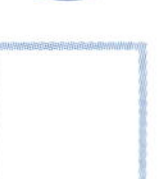

great!

Exits

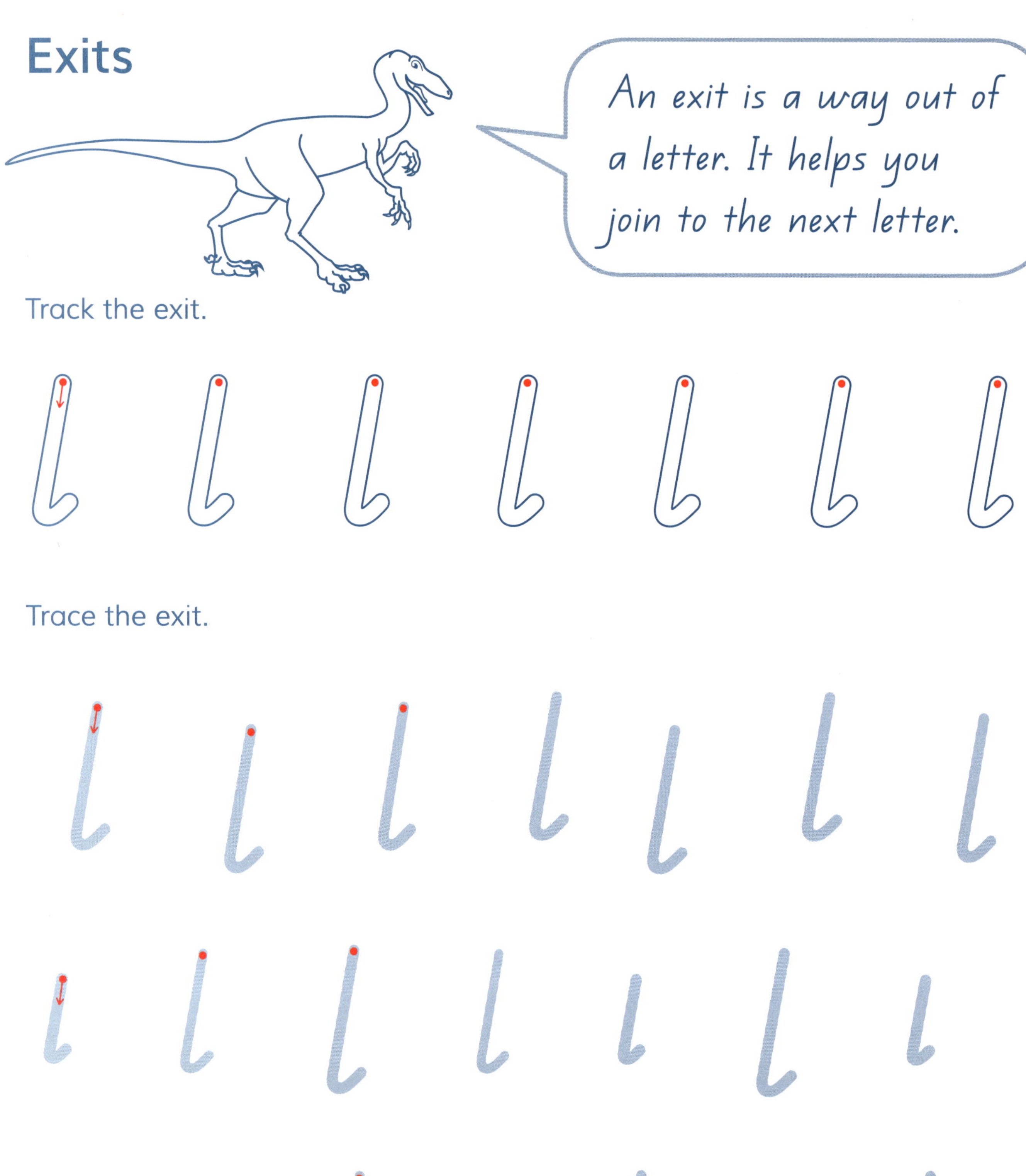

Track the exit.

Trace the exit.

Practise the exit. Trace and complete the line.

Exit-only letters

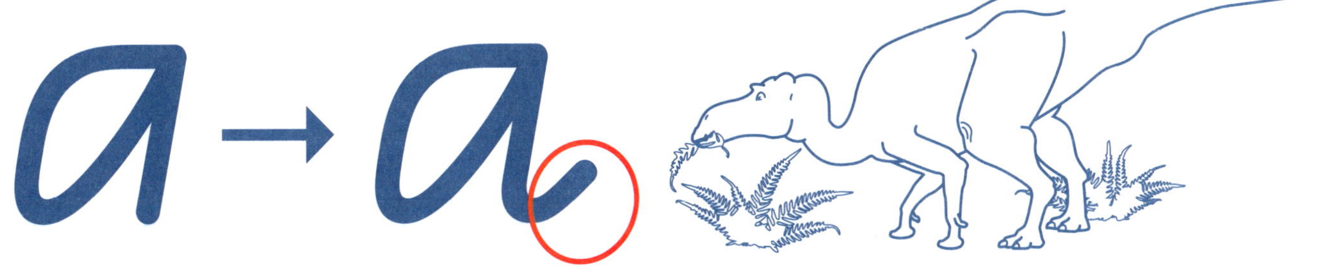

Circle the exits.

a h k l

Complete the line, then trace and copy.

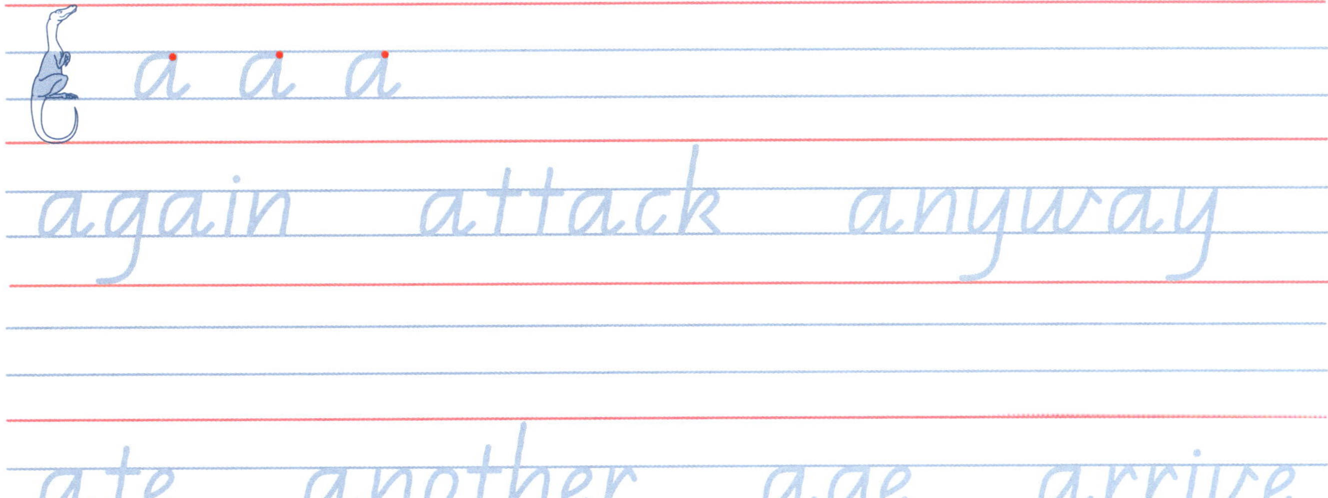

Copy this word. Circle the letter with the exit.

Archaeopteryx

Complete the line, then trace and copy.

h h h

head hear heavy half

hungry hatch happen

hardly happier hairy

Complete the line, then trace and copy.

k k k

knock keep knee kill

kept kindly knew key

Circle your best k.

Complete the line, then trace and copy.

The letter 't'

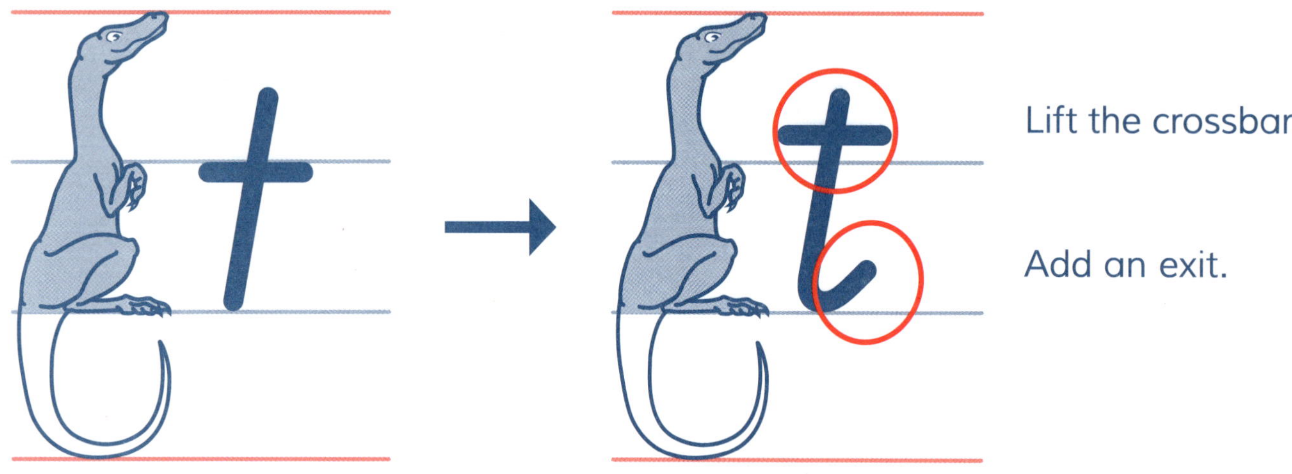

Lift the crossbar.

Add an exit.

Complete the line, then trace and copy.

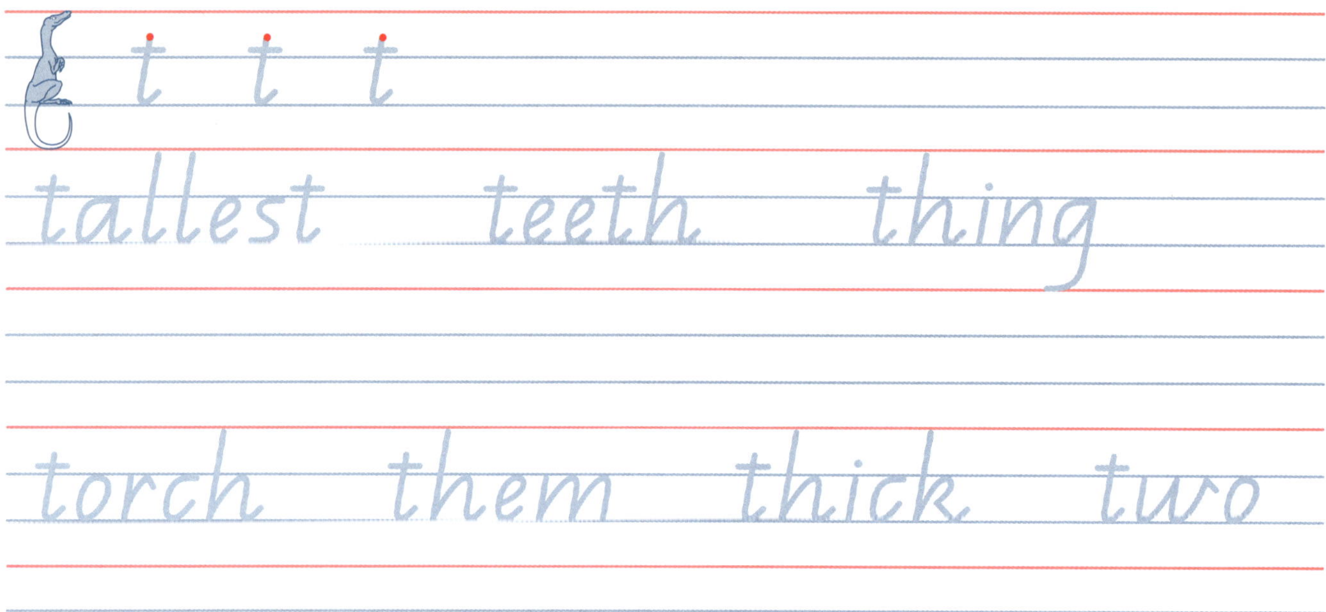

Use exits to write the dinosaur name.

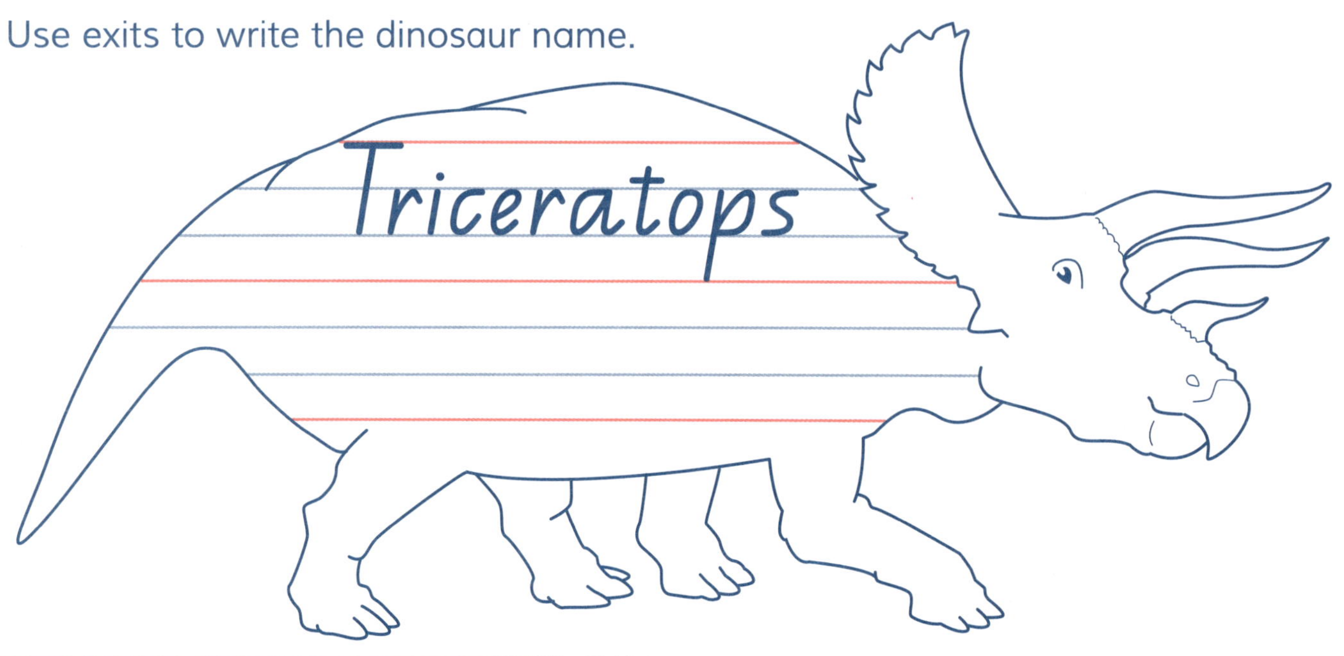

These letters already have exits. Circle the exits.

c d e

Copy the text. Circle your neatest word.

Triceratops were plant

eaters. Their babies

walked in the middle

of the herd to keep safe.

Self-assessment

My exit letters:

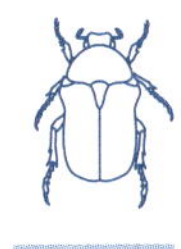

need more practice.

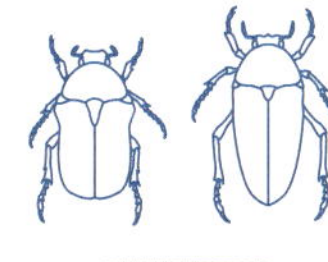

are getting better.

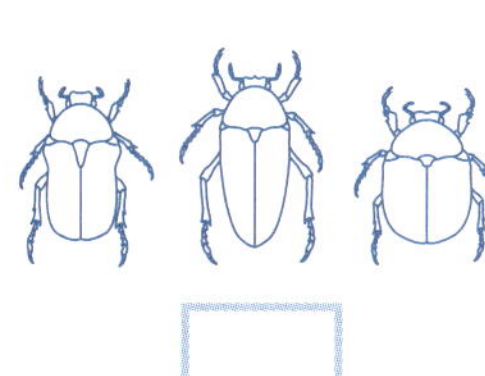

are looking great!

Rounded entries

An entry is a way into a letter. It helps you join to the letter.

Track the entry.

Trace the entry.

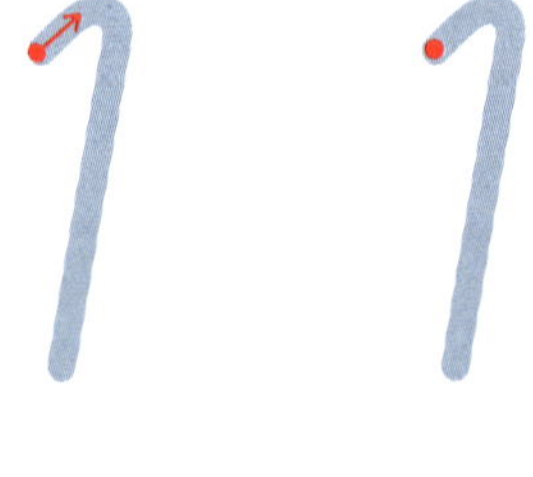      

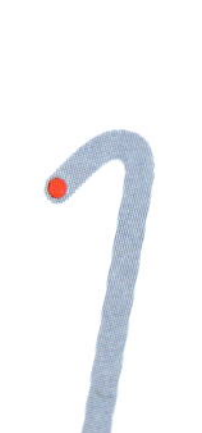    

Practise the entry. Trace and complete the line.

Rounded-entry letters

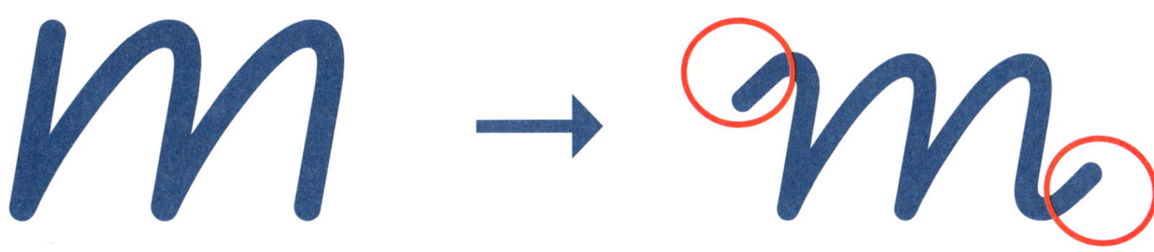

All of these letters, except r, have both an entry and an exit. Circle any entries and exits you can find.

Complete the line, then trace and copy.

m m m

middle most matter

more mean moment

How many exits in this word?

themselves

Complete the line, then trace and copy.

n n n

nothing nibbled noise

nose nest nine not

notice nowhere never

Complete the line, then trace and copy.

r r r

ready reach rattled

rumbled roared round

Complete the line, then trace and copy.

Trace and copy. Circle your neatest word.

Arky is an Archaeopteryx

dinosaur. She has bright

colours and wide wings.

Circle the rounded-entry letter that was not practised above.

m n r x

Colour the wedges.

dinosaur

List the body letters you practised. Write each letter only once.

get.ga/PMWA21

Pointed entries

Some letters have rounded entries.
Other letters have pointed entries.
They help you join to the letter.

Track the entry.

    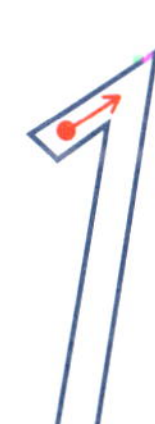  

Trace the entry.

   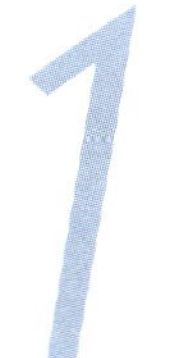

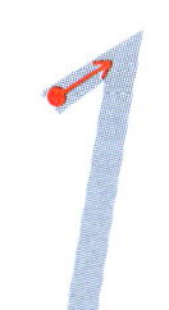     

Practise the entry. Trace and complete the line.

Pointed-entry letters

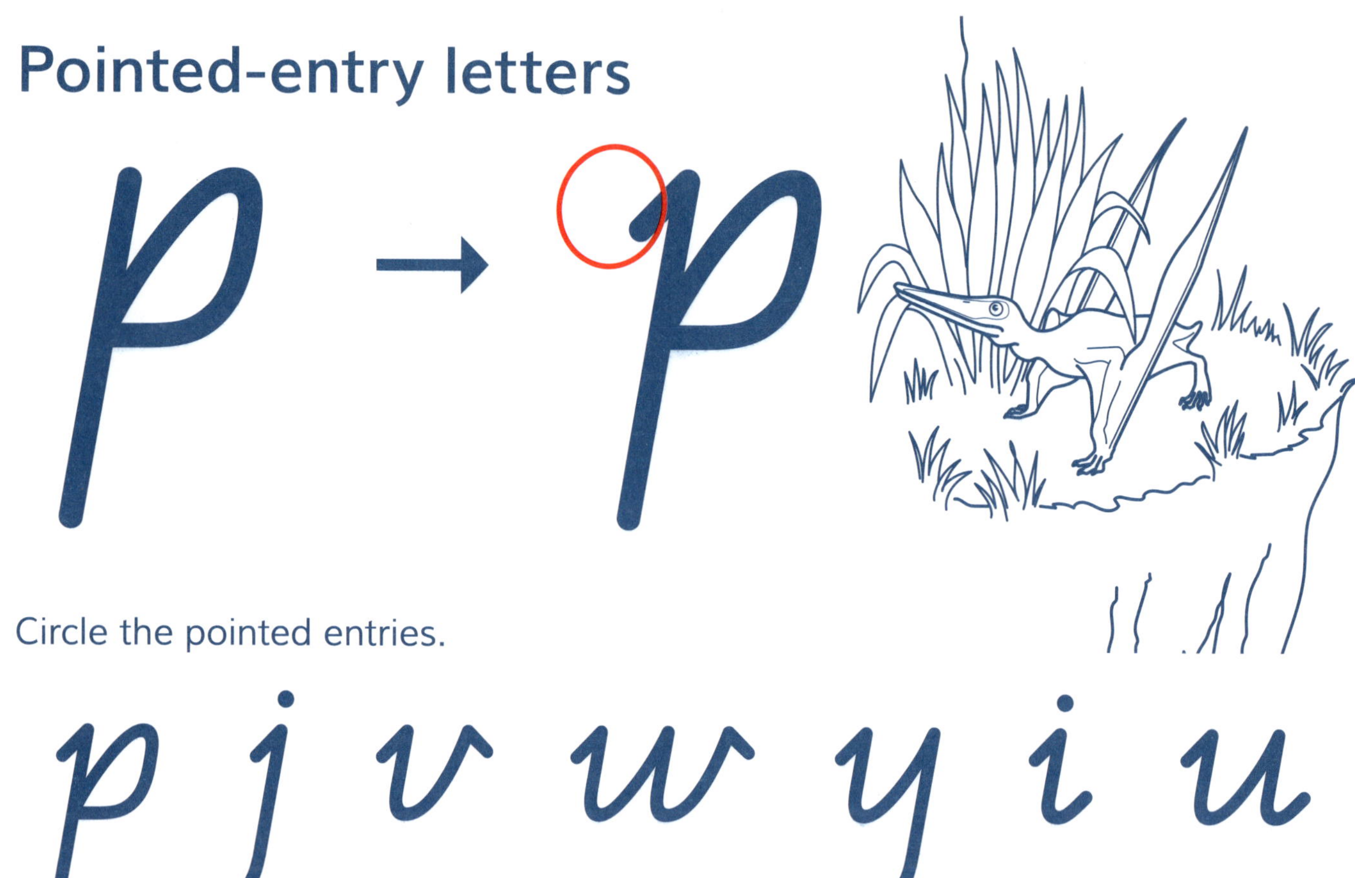

Circle the pointed entries.

p j v w y i u

Complete the line, then trace and copy.

p p p

pushed pleased power

past people peep part

pretend pair prickles

Complete the line, then trace and copy.

j j j

jaws just jets joins

jumped jacket jam

jeans jelly jug juice

Trace and copy these patterns.

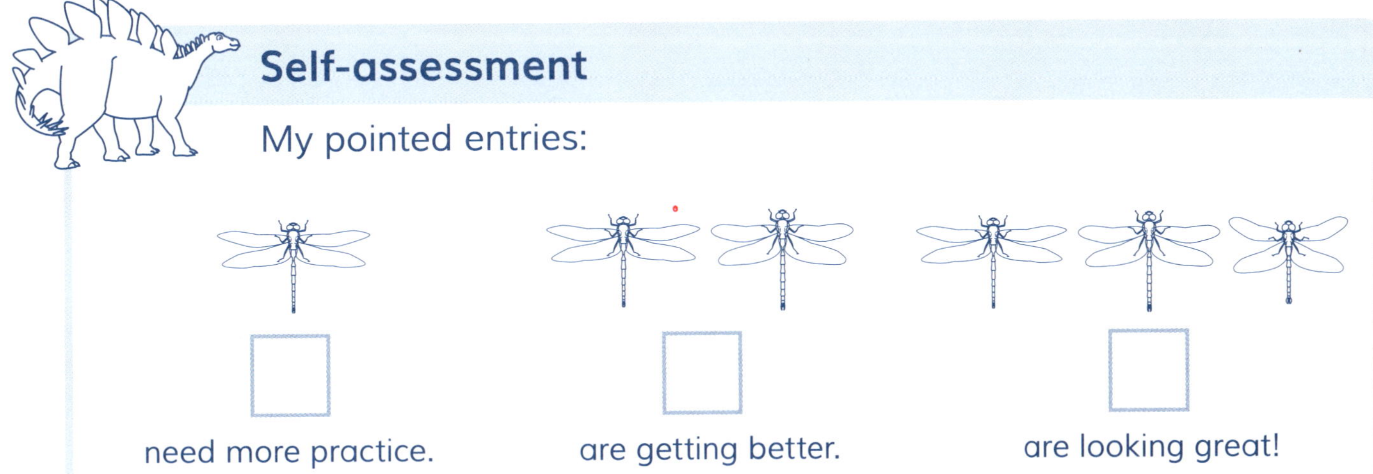

Complete the line, then trace and copy.

v v v

volcano village voice

valley vase vegetable

vest vinegar vowel

Complete the line, then trace and copy.

w w w

wide weather wonder

waiting walking want

would world which

Complete the line, then trace and copy.

y y y

yard yesterday year

yet you're you've yes

yawn yells yolk you

QUIZ

1 List the body letters from the activity at the top of this page. Write each letter only once.

2 How many wedges? yesterday

The letters 'i' and 'u' have a pointed entry and an exit.

Circle the entry and the exit.

i u

Complete the line, then trace and copy.

i i i

idea important indeed

isn't ice insect into

inside invitation iron

Trace and copy these exit and entry patterns.

iıiı ıııı i·i·i·i

uuu u|u|u uouou

Complete the line, then trace and copy.

u u u

under use unpack

unlock underneath

understand undo

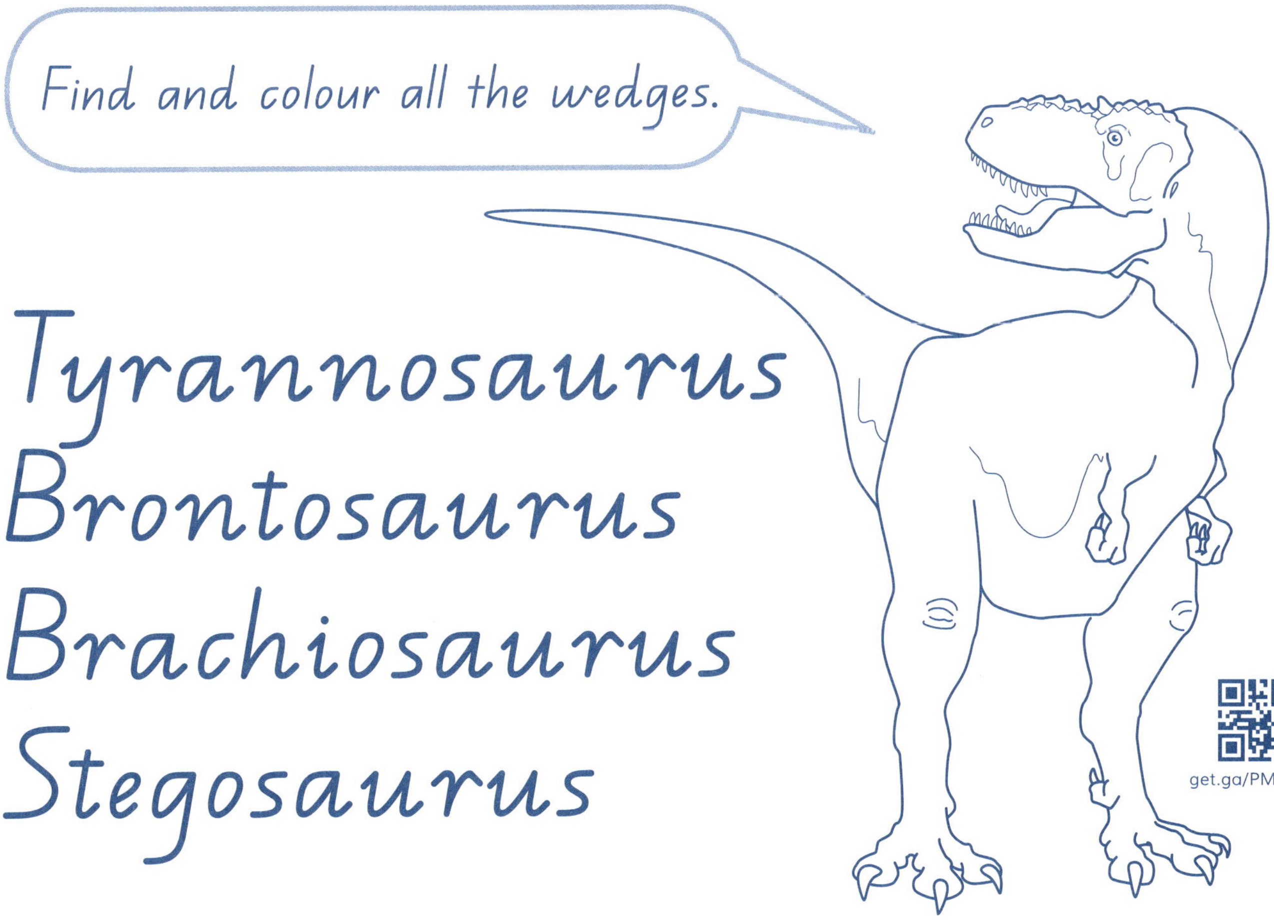

Find and colour all the wedges.

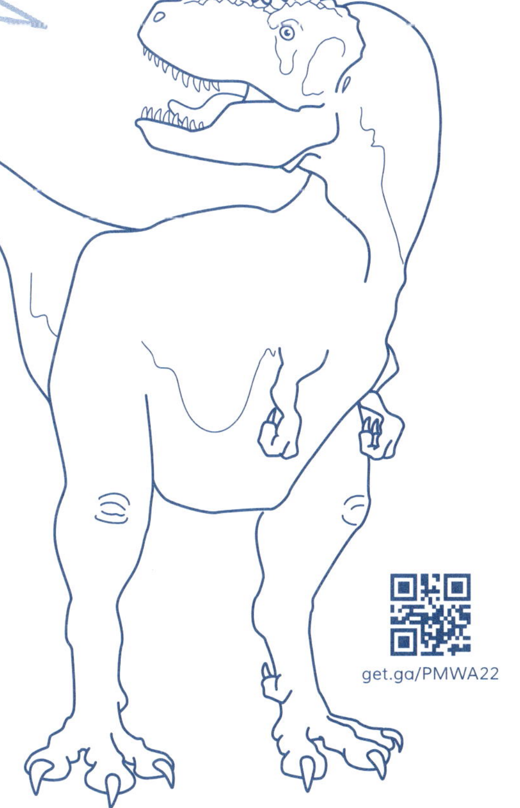

Tyrannosaurus
Brontosaurus
Brachiosaurus
Stegosaurus

get.ga/PMWA22

The letter 'f'

f is now a head,
body and tail letter.
Complete the line, then trace and copy.
forest flowers flap
ferns feeding flight
faster frightened fled

The letter 'z'

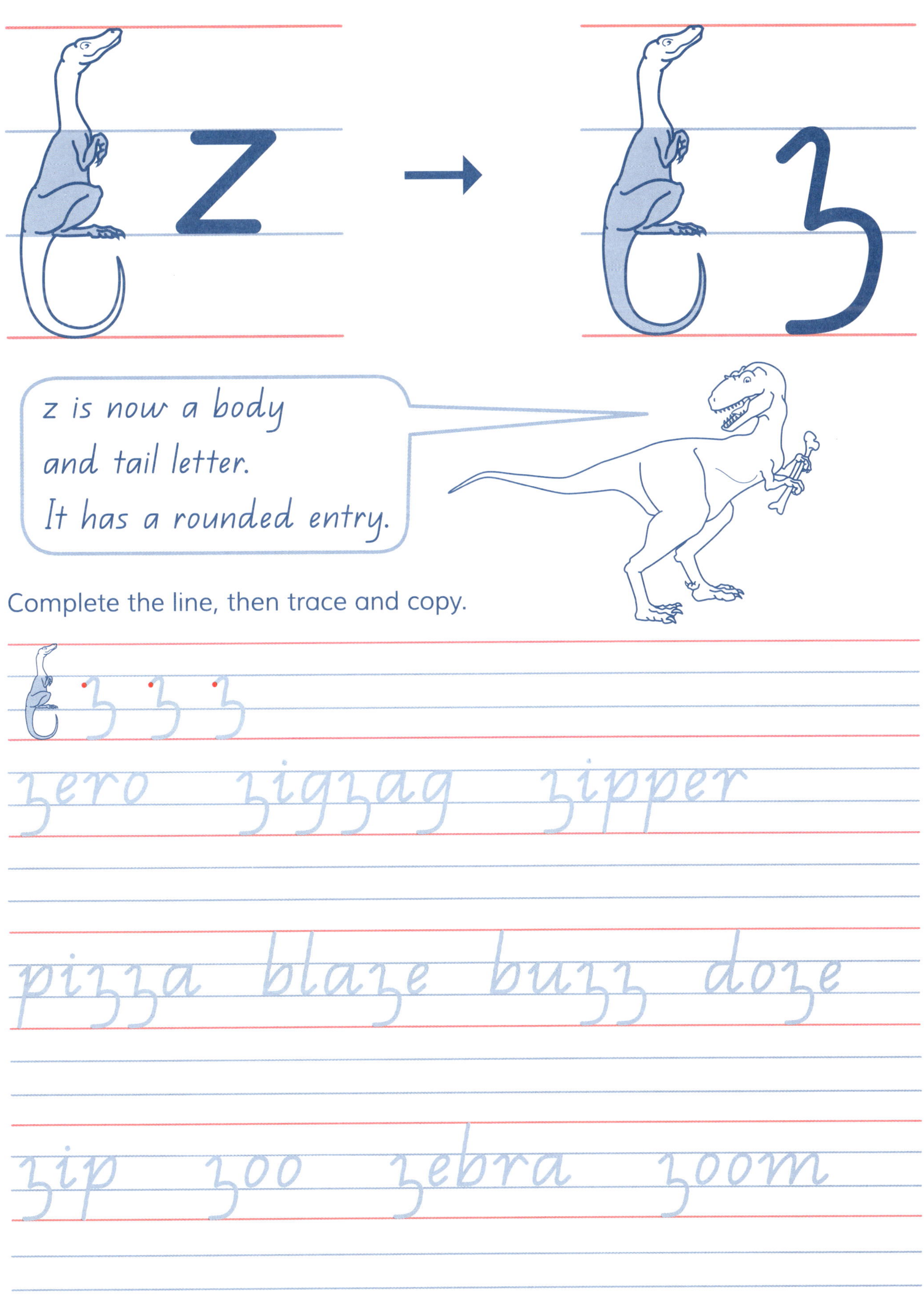
z
z is now a body
and tail letter.
It has a rounded entry.
Complete the line, then trace and copy.
z z z
zero zigzag zipper
pizza blaze buzz doze
zip zoo zebra zoom

Practising exits and entries

Trace and copy.

Trace and copy the book title.

A Bad Day for

Little Dinosaur

Trace and copy the list of animals
Little Dinosaur meets.

beetle crab

Big Dinosaur

Trace Little Dinosaur's shape.

Practise the alphabet with exits and entries.

Trace and copy.

a b c d e f g h i j k

l m n o p q r s t u

v w x y z

8 letters have not changed from the Beginner's Alphabet. Circle them above, then write them below.

Write the letters of the alphabet under the correct heading.

Exit-only letters (7)

Rounded-entry letters (4)

Pointed-entry letters (7)

Letters that change (3)

3

Write the 5 letters from the alphabet that don't appear above.

Copy the text using exits and entries.

Pterosaurs were flying

reptiles. They swooped

low over waterways to

snap up fish with their

narrow jaws. Their

wings were made of

skin and muscle.

List letters from the text on the opposite page. List each letter only once.

Rounded-entry letters

Pointed-entry letters

Colour the wedges.

get.ga/PMWA23

waterways

List body letters from the text on the opposite page.
List each letter only once.

Self-assessment

My handwriting on the opposite page is:

getting there. very good. fantastic!

Practise the alphabet with exits and entries.

aA bB cC dD eE fF

gG hH iI jJ kK lL

mM nN oO pP qQ

rR sS tT uU vV

wW xX yY zZ

List the 7 lower-case letters that finish with this clockwise movement.

Introducing diagonal joins

Try these exit patterns.

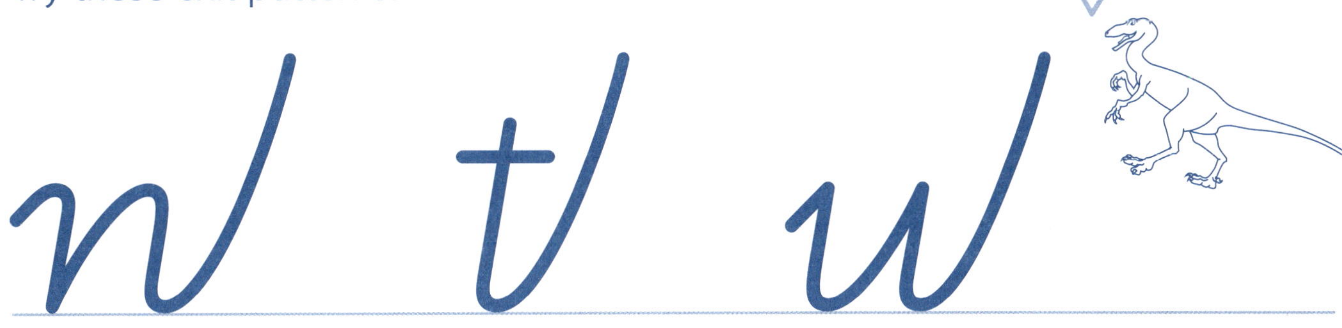

Try sweeping these exits high.

Trace and copy these exit patterns.

Diagonal joins to pointed entries

Practise these diagonal joins to pointed entries.

Diagonal joins to rounded entries

Practise these diagonal joins to rounded entries.

am an ar ax az cr

dr em en er ex im

in ir ix iz mm mn

nn tr um un ur ux

Write these words using diagonal joins.

air jaw tip bin

Diagonal joins to head and body letters

Practise these diagonal joins.

ab ak al at ch ck ct

eb el et ib il it lb lt

mb nt th tt ub ul ut

Choose a letter pair from above to make a word on each line below.

b_____ f_____ h_____

l_____ p_____ n_____

Diagonal joins to e and o

ne

You may need to lower the exit of the letter joining to e.

ho

Sweep up to the top of o, then move anti-clockwise.

Practise these tricky diagonal joins.

ae ao ce co de do ee eo

he ho ie le lo me mo

ne no te to ue ko ke

Practising diagonal joins

Remember how to make diagonal joins?
Practice makes perfect!

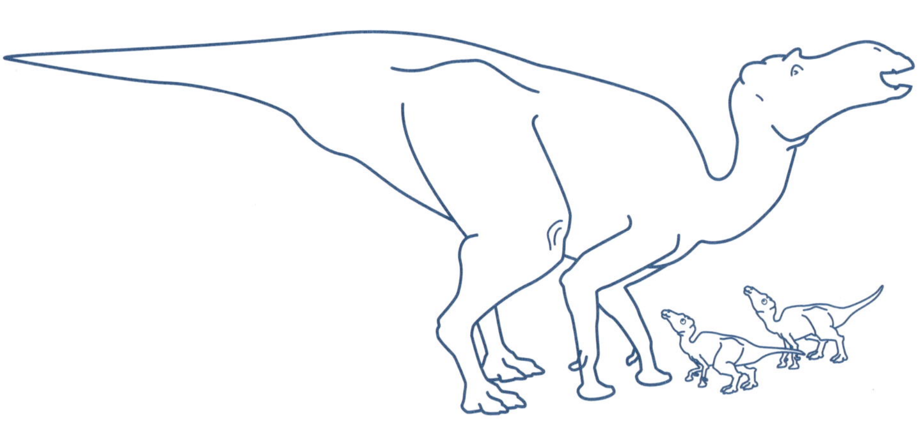

get.ga/PMWA24

Add the letters to make a diagonal join. Then practise the join.

d + r =

a + u =

m + o =

l + y =

h + e =

e + v =

i + p =

n + t =

Join these letters and letter pairs, then complete the line.

me + n =

de + n =

ne + w =

l + et =

m + et =

t + ub =

n + ut =

n + et =

th + e =

h + um =

h + em =

k + ey =

d + im =

m + um =

Write the alphabet with diagonal joins.

abcdefghijklmnopqrstuv

wxyz

Write these words with diagonal joins.

time her him like it

then they them tell

quite put pull pink

peep pile nine little

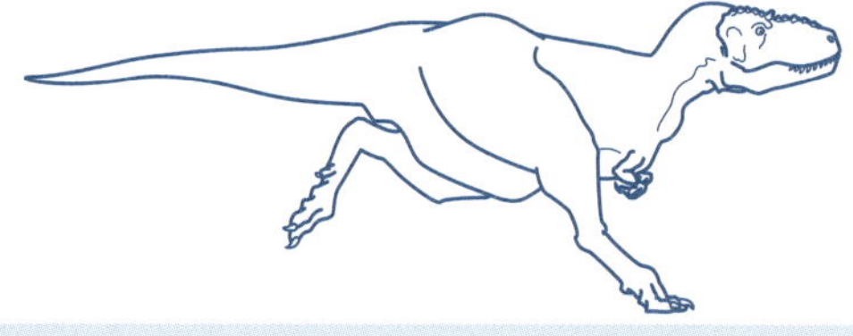

Complete the line, practising the diagonal join.

ly ly

Rewrite the word, using any diagonal joins and adding -ly.

careful + ly → carefully

quiet + ly →

quick + ly →

loud + ly →

soft + ly →

Complete the line, practising the diagonal join.

er er

Rewrite the word, using any diagonal joins and adding -er.

long + er →

strong + er →

loud + er →

fast + er →

Add -ly or -er to these words.

bright →

deep →

green →

lean →

own →

part →

poor →

thick →

tall →

short →

Self-assessment

My diagonal joins:

☐ need more practice.

☐ are not bad!

☐ look great!

The letter 'q'

Write these words containing the letter **'q'**.

squid equal quick

square quiet queen

question quilt quiz

Trace and copy these **q** patterns.

quq q|q| |q|q

Capital letters

Capital letters never join to lower-case letters. Copy these words.

Australia Queensland

January June July

Tuesday Sunday Friday

Write your name using any diagonal joins.

Copy these names.

get.ga/PMWA25

Kai Sam Henry Marta

Circle the word on the page that shows your neatest handwriting.

Have you read these PM dinosaur books?

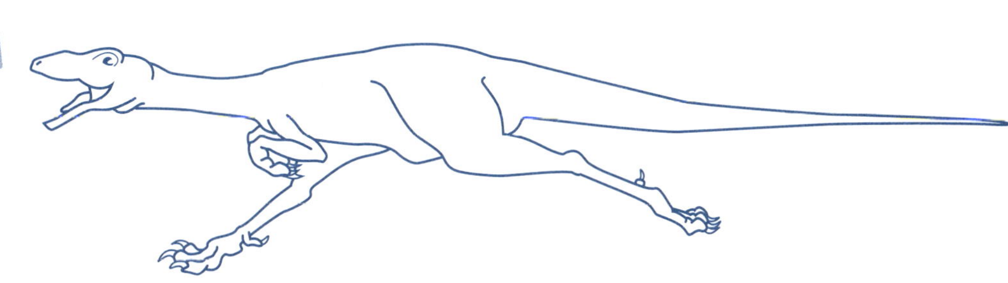

Write each title, adding the necessary capital letters.
The number tells you how many are needed.

4 gorgo meets her match

2 brave triceratops

3 pterosaur's long flight

3 the dinosaur chase

3 little dinosaur escapes

Numbers

Practise numbers using diagonal joins

63 sixty-three

72 seventy-two

81 eighty-one

39 thirty-nine

27 twenty-seven

Choose a number from above to match each clue.

largest number	smallest number	number with three tens	even number

Solve each maths problem using words. The answer will be a numeral from the opposite page. Each numeral is used twice.

80 + 1 =

50 + 13 =

20 + 7 =

60 + 3 =

70 + 2 =

20 + 19 =

62 + 10 =

70 + 11 =

10 + 17 =

30 + 9 =

Write the numbers above in order from smallest to biggest.

______, ______, ______, ______, ______,

______, ______, ______, ______, ______

Teacher observation guide

Student is: left-handed ☐ right-handed ☐

Student demonstrates correct posture, paper position and pencil grip. ☐

Student is stroking from top to bottom. ☐

Student is stroking from left to right. ☐

Student is tracking accurately using starting dots and arrows. ☐

Student is tracing accurately using starting dots and arrows. ☐

Student forms the Beginner's Alphabet with accuracy. ☐

Student uses head, body and tail character to describe the spatial properties of letters. ☐

Student understands the four basic movement groups to which letters belong (straight-line, clockwise, anti-clockwise, double-rotation). ☐

Student can identify and colour wedges. ☐

Student can copy a complete sentence with accuracy. ☐

Student can identify entries (pointed or rounded) and exits. ☐

Student forms diagonal joins to pointed entries with accuracy. ☐

Student forms diagonal joins to rounded entries with accuracy. ☐

Student forms diagonal joins to head and body letters with accuracy. ☐

Student forms tricky joins to e and o with accuracy. ☐

Student writes the Modern Cursive forms of f, t and z with accuracy. ☐

Student can identify when a diagonal join is required. ☐

Student can identify when a capital letter is required. ☐

Student can write the numerals 0–100. ☐

Student can self-assess with accuracy. ☐

Notes:

....

....

....

Date: ....

CERTIFICATE

get.ga/PMWC3